Sylvia St Jean.

Be Happy!!

You are loved.!!

D0952884

SECRETS OF HAPPINESS

ONE FOR EACH DAY OF THE MONTH

J. DONALD WALTERS

Hardbound Edition
First Printing 1993

Illustration Copyright © 1993 Crystal Clarity, Publishers

Text Copyright © 1989 J. Donald Walters

ISBN 1-56589-025-6

PRINTED IN HONG KONG

Crystal Clarity
PUBLISHERS
14618 Tyler Foote Road, Nevada City, CA 95959
1 (800) 424-1055

A seed thought is offered for every day of the month. Begin a day at the appropriate date. Repeat the saying several times: first out loud, then softly, then in a whisper, and then only mentally. With each repetition, allow the words to become absorbed ever more deeply into your subconscious. Thus, gradually, you will acquire as complete an understanding as one might gain from a year's course in the subject. At this point, indeed, the truths set forth here will have become your own.

Keep the book open at the pertinent page throughout the day. Refer to it occasionally during moments of leisure. Relate the saying as often as possible to real situations in your life.

Then at night, before you go to bed, repeat the thought several times more. While falling asleep, carry the words into your subconscious, absorbing their positive influence into your whole being. Let it become thereby an integral part of your normal consciousness.

Day

1

The Secret of Happiness

is the innocent enjoyment

of simple things.

Day

2

The Secret of Happiness

is seeing one's work as service.

Day

3

The Secret of Happiness

is a smile of comfort

to the sorrowful.

The Secret of Happiness

is a heart kept open

to the stranger.

Day

4

Day

5

The Secret of Happiness

is working with other people's realities,

with their natures as they are,

and not trying to force them

into a mold of one's own making.

The Secret of Happiness

is including other people's happiness

in one's own.

Day

6

Day

7

The Secret of Happiness

is understanding that friendship

is more precious that mere things,

more precious than getting

one's own way, more precious

than being right in situations

where true principles are not at stake.

The Secret of Happiness

is accepting whatever comes,

with an attitude of calm,

inner freedom.

Day

8

Day

9

The Secret of Happiness

is finding love through giving love,

rather than through receiving it.

The Secret of Happiness

is a pure heart,

empty of malice

and self-seeking.

Day

10

Day
11

The Secret of Happiness

is the determination to *be* happy always,

rather than wait for outer circumstances

to make one happy.

The Secret of Happiness

is even-mindedness

through all the storms of life.

Day

12

Day

13

The Secret of Happiness

is living in, but not for,

the moment —

in the Eternal Now.

Day

14

The Secret of Happiness

is giving up personal attachments,

recognizing that nothing and no one

truly belongs to us, since all is God's.

Day

15

The Secret of Happiness

is reverence for all life.

The Secret of Happiness

is loyalty to one's own,

then gradually expanding that loyalty

to include all beings as one's own.

Day

16

Day

17

The Secret of Happiness

is a humble heart,

free from pretensions,

aware that nothing man can do

is of everlasting importance.

Day

18

The Secret of Happiness

is worshiping God everywhere,

in everything.

Day

19

The Secret of Happiness

is laughing with others, not at them.

The Secret of Happiness

is kindness, seeing others

as extensions of one's own self.

The Secret of Happiness

is laughing with others, not at them.

The Secret of Happiness

is kindness, seeing others

as extensions of one's own self.

Day

20

Day

21

The Secret of Happiness

is doing joyfully and willingly

whatever needs to be done.

Day

22

The Secret of Happiness

is the desire to learn,

rather than to teach.

Day

23

The Secret of Happiness

is the ability to congratulate oneself

happily on one's own unimportance

while others vie together for supremacy.

The Secret of Happiness

is understanding

that man's highest duty

is to love.

Day

24

Day

25

The Secret of Happiness

is smiling with the heart and eyes,

not merely with the lips.

Day

26

The Secret of Happiness

is seeking rather to help others

than to be helped by them.

Day

27

The Secret of Happiness

is strengthening others' faith

in themselves,

and in their own high potential.

The Secret of Happiness

is being grateful

for the hurts one receives,

for they are channels

of understanding

and wisdom.

Day

28

Day

29

The Secret of Happiness

is relinquishing

the sense of "I" and "mine."

The Secret of Happiness

is a heart reaching out to embrace

all mankind as brothers and sisters.

Day

30

The Secret of Happiness

is love.

Day

31

OTHER BOOKS BY J. DONALD WALTERS

Hardbound

SECRETS OF SUCCESS $5.95

SECRETS OF FRIENDSHIP $5.95

SECRETS OF INNER PEACE $5.95

SECRETS OF LOVE $5.95

Soft Cover

AFFIRMATIONS FOR SELF-HEALING This inspirational book offers insights into 52 different qualities such as willpower, forgiveness, and openness, through the use of affirmations and prayer. $7.95

MONEY MAGNETISM: *How to Attract What You Need When You Need It* This book offers fresh, new insights on proven ways of increasing money magnetism without making it a burden on one's peace of mind. $7.95

THE ART OF SUPPORTIVE LEADERSHIP An invaluable tool for anyone in a position of responsibility who views management in terms of shared accomplishment rather than personal advancement. $7.95